dancing into unlimited possibilities

dancing
into
unlimited possibilities

Kimberly E. Sutton

Kimberly E. Sutton
Chicago

First Edition
Printed in the United States of America

Library of Congress
ISBN 13: 978-0-9854085-5-8

CoverArt:
Heather Pettersen, "Dancing in the Sun"
http://www.heatherpettersen.com
Cover Design and Interior Layout: RL Johnson

Ready to Dance

(An Introduction)

Layer by layer I am stepping out of this old skin
Bold...Brave...Unyielding
STRONG.

I feel like a BUTTERFLY that has just discovered its wings
So beautiful
So free

One with my Soul
One with my Destiny
One with the Horizons of Possibilities that are Waiting for Me

I didn't know that it could be like this
I never realized that I could FLY.

As a writer I draw upon a myriad of things for inspiration; sometimes it's the lyrics in a song, a personal relationship, or a particular life experience. This entire book is based upon these pieces of inspiration. This is a labor of love for me. I wanted this book to be the very best representation of Self that it could be.

The emotions represented in this book are UNIVERSAL. **I know that you are going to FEEL what I am talking about.**

Always,
Kimberly

Dedicated To...

The Trinity – Thank You, God, for the gift of words and emotions. Thank You for Your sweet and precious son Jesus. Thank You for the Holy Spirit who calms all my fears.

My Mother – You are so brilliant and brave! You are the epitome of what it means to be a woman of grace, intelligence, strength and character. Thank you for instilling in me a love of reading and books. I simply could not ask for a more amazing Mother and Friend. I love you very much!

My Dearest Friends – Jolynn, Christine, Michelle, Khalilah, Getty, Stephanie, Dione, Yolanda and Tamico. Thank you for being so incredibly supportive.

Alpha Kappa Alpha Sorority, Incorporated – Especially Sandra, Khalilah, Stephanie, Dachia, Bernadette and Joni!!! I also want to give a very special dedication to Christine. You are so much more than a Soror to me...you're Family! I am so thankful that I was able to meet you – your friendship means the world to me.

Table of Contents

I
STORIES OF FAITH

II
BROWN SUGAR

III
BitterSWEET

IV
UNLIMITED POSSIBILITIES

I

Stories of Faith

Awesome Virgins LikeFire Beliefs Peace Forged Sanctity Thank Mic Teach Hallelujah FAITH STORIES None Perfect

I do not have a scientific explanation for how the universe was formed or how we as human beings came to exist. There is no mathematical equation that I can point you towards that details the formation of mountaintops and blue skies...the wonder of a baby's laughter...the feeling of absolute amazement and joy at the feel of the warmth of the sun. It might be deemed as a simplistic view, but I choose to believe that the Creator is the source for all that I have listed, and so much more!

I know that many people do not believe in a Higher Being – this book is by no means an attempt to coerce or convert people into believing in God. Faith and spirituality are an essential part of my life, and I am thankful for everything that He has done for me. Stories of Faith is my way of giving thanks.

Virgin to the Mic

I step up to the mike…

A little hesitant
Legs shaking
Sweaty palms
Butterflies in my stomach

I am petrified that I will not do the WORDS justice
That when I begin to speak, the phrases won't
resonate with the POWER they were intended to wield

I do not want to belittle this gift
I want to pay it the Honor and Respect that it deserves

My voice shakes
My vocal chords struggle as the syllables attempt to
make their escape
Then something happens inside my Soul
The anxiety fades and the Creativity flows
The Force inside of me takes over

The words are fighting their way to freedom
They will not be contained
They must be heard

I speak S L O W L Y
I am trying to connect with the audience…trying to be
sure that they are in sync with me
But after awhile, the WORDS TAKE OVER
I no longer see the people

I am ONE with the words and the memories that they evoke
One with the Memories that form a timeline of my Journey ...
A journey of love, grace, fear, pain and HOPE
A journey that is composed of so many different EXPERIENCES

In the end, the WORDS are ALL THAT MATTER
They have wrapped me up in their embrace and will not let me go

Inspiration

The memory of my first Open Mic night; also the feelings that writing evokes within me. I truly believe that God blessed me with this gift, and I want to honor Him in every way possible.

Teach Me

I am ready to be a scholar of Your Word
To embrace the patience and selflessness that is the
embodiment of Your Son
Show Me

Show me how to speak words that heal and unite, not
hurt or divide
Give me a clean heart
A heart that is ready and open to serve
A heart that is full of Your Love

Allow me to dwell in Your presence...just to sit at Your
feet is an honor I do not deserve

My life is available to You
Without You, I don't know where I'd be
I was lost and stumbling around a barren
desert...bereft...feeling so alone
And You came and Found me...
Carried me from an abyss so deep that I had no clue
how to find my way back to You
Lord God, You loved me in spite of my many flaws

Reveal Yourself to me Lord
Show me Your will for my life

My soul has an eternal thirst for You, Father
Like the waves upon the sea, I need You
I long for Your Presence
I cannot make it through this life without You
Guide me, Lord

Teach me
Teach me to walk in Your Will...to live out Your Word
Allow neither pride nor willful disobedience to
separate me from You

I TRUST You implicitly, God
With my soul
...my heart
...my life
With the very ESSENCE of who I am

Take me Lord and mold me as You see fit
I need You so deeply
Teach me, Father
Teach me to be a servant

Teach me to be more like YOU

Inspiration

God is waiting patiently for us to acknowledge His divine presence. He is waiting for us to stop struggling and trust Him.

Mantra

I trust God.
I believe that He is the Supreme Source.
I have Faith that the Heavenly Father will
never give me more than I can bear.

Head Over Heels

I am so in love with You
In spite of my lack of worthiness, You LOVE me
Though I have sinned in word and deed, You sacrificed
Your only Son for me

Your love for me is unconditional

Even on my worst days Your feelings for me are
constant
When storms are raging all around me, You are a
steady port
I am reassured by Your presence
Comforted that You will never give me more than I can
bear

I want to be a vessel for what You represent

Take me Lord and mold me into what You want me to
be
Use me as You see fit
Give me a clean heart
Regulate my thoughts and words

Grant me the sanctity and grace of Your presence

When I stumble and fall, give me the faith and
strength to rise again
Stronger
Wiser
My feet firmly planted in Your word

I love You with everything I am
You Alone Are Sufficient

I am so in love with You, Lord

Inspiration

A mighty and awesome God.
There is truly no one like Him.

Your relationship with CHRIST
is not dependent upon a building

Awesome (None Like You)

In this entire Earth, there is nobody like You
Nobody that can care for us
Soothe us
Love us

You are so awesome
It is only by Your love, grace and mercy that we are
saved
It is Your grace and mercy that embodies us with the
strength and courage to forgive

I am so grateful for Your love
So grateful for this life that You have granted me

If I had the gift of one million words, it would not be
adequate to express my love for You
You are just that good
You are just that beautiful
You are just that awesome
You are just that Faithful
Your love for us is just that great

In all of this Earth, there is NONE like You

Inspiration

The realization that God's love, grace and mercy is
never-ending. What a wonderful testament to the love
that He has for us!

Sanctity of Beliefs

I believe in all that is good and true
I believe that God will never give us more than we can
handle
I believe that He loves us in a way that we cannot fully
comprehend or appreciate
I believe that He protects us from all matters of harm
and danger – even if that includes ourselves

I believe in REDEMPTION
I believe that everyone deserves a second chance
I believe in Heart, Spirit and Soul
I believe that we show people who we are by how we
treat others each and every day

I believe that a sunrise is the dawning of a new day –
A new day and a new chance to be a better person

I believe in the beauty of dreams
I believe in the spirit of hope
I believe in the sacredness of friendship
I believe in the power of words
I believe in the purity of love and the strength of
convictions

I believe that we are blessed

Inspiration

The value of beliefs. If you do not know what you believe in, you are in real trouble. The lack of a belief structure is why so many people are lost...filled with emptiness inside; constantly searching for something or someone to make them feel whole. Life is sometimes difficult, but it is beautiful, too. What a blessing to be allowed another day to be a better person...to bring joy to someone's life...to laugh...to live... It is an honor and a privilege to be granted life!

Mantra

I am connected to the
Universe and the Creator.
I serve a divine purpose.
I truly believe that I am blessed.

Thank You

Thank You for Your many blessings
Thank You for grace, mercy and peace of mind
Thank You for Inspiration
Thank You for Love, Life and Music
Thank You for this Gift

Inspiration

Gratitude. Thank you to the Creator for granting me the gift of creative expression. Thank you to you, the Reader, for taking this journey with me...

Perfect Peace

I can feel the arms of the Lord wrapped around me
He soothes me and calms my spirit
I can feel Him telling me peace be still...and in Him I
find strength

I can feel the words of our God whispered into my ear
He gives me the gift of words...the gift of melody...
In Him, I have found joy and serenity

Through all of my many journeys, He has been with
me every step of the way
He grants me free will to make my own decisions
Sometimes I do mess up, but when I do, He picks me
up and encourages me to keep going
He loves all of the pain and hurt away

Through Him I am stronger than when I am alone
When I trust and obey Him, everything is fine

What a tranquil feeling it is to have Him in my life
He gives me Perfect Peace

Inspiration

God, Adonai, Elohim, Jehovah, Creator, Yahweh, El Shaddai... All across the world He is called by many different names, but His grace and mercy is the same regardless of what language you speak, or what you call Him.

FAITH
even in
the midst of
uncertainty

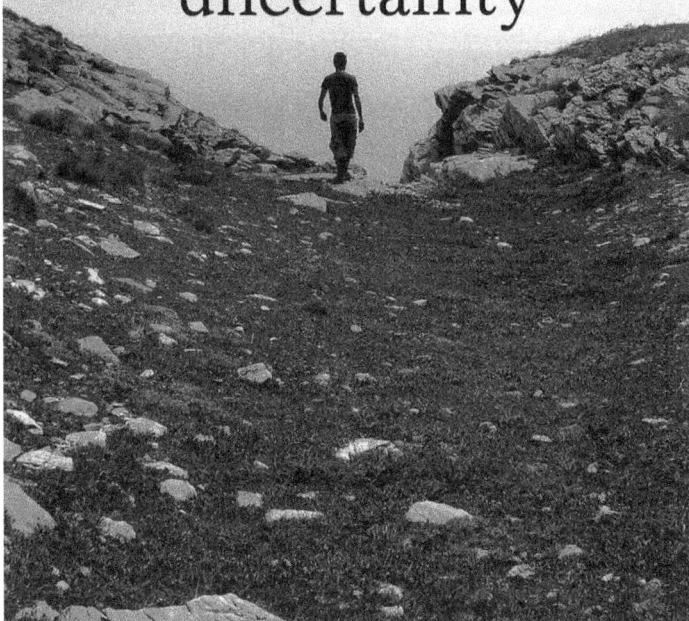

Forged in the Fire (Hallelujah!)

I look back at past experiences and all I can say is
Hallelujah!!!
So many times I could have been broken, but instead I
emerged from the Flames as a New Person

At times I thought the Pain would Swallow me whole
That I would drown in a lake of tears
The weights of sorrow and defeat were like Shackles
around my Soul
Fear Consumed Me

H A L L E L U J A H !

Sometimes I've had to fight off external enemies;
Sometimes I have been my OWN worst enemy
So many times I could have been broken....
So many times I WAS broken
Lack of Faith causing me to be tossed about like a rag
doll in a storm

H A L L E L U J A H !

We have to be thankful for the occurrences in life that
Mold Us
Shape Us
Forge us into better Men and Women

If we are patient, there is a MANIFESTATION that
takes place...
He Is There
If we can just be still enough to recognize it....

He Is There

He is waiting for us to recognize His omnipotence
He will not leave us Alone with our Fears
Selah!
He will NOT leave us Alone with our Fears

His Embrace and Love can Comfort like no other
From the Fire, there can be Peace
From the Fire, there can be Joy

H A L L E L U J A H !

I Was Forged In The Fire.

H A L L E L U J A H !

I Am Free!

Inspiration

There is immense value in experiencing a storm – valuable lessons to be learned about yourself and others. Don't be afraid to meet the storm head-on; you will emerge stronger and more powerful than before!

Mantra

I believe that there is value in
every life experience.
I know that I am capable of rising to the
challenge – regardless of the circumstance.
I am a Conqueror.

II

Brown Sugar

Girl Soul
Thickness Pimp
Bond
soulfree

Revolution
Side BROWN SUGAR Love Infinite
Black-Hand
Black Consolidation G.A.W Bloodlines
HSLFLSH/SELFISH Word
BEAUTIFUL

*B*eing birthed as a Black woman has brought me an immeasurable amount of joy and with that, periods of pain. Through it all, I LOVE being a Black woman.

I love the varied skin tones, shapes, ethnicities, dialects and EXPERIENCES that I encounter when I meet other people of color. I love the foundation of strength and courage that our history is built upon.

Brown Sugar is a story of Love, Culture, Responsibility, Faith and PRIDE. In a way, Brown Sugar is my love letter (in poetry format) to all people of color.

BEAUTIFUL/SELFISH

How Beautiful are the feet of our Ancestors that have come before us.

The ones that plowed the fields until their feet were riddled and sore with blisters
The ones that endured the pain of the lashings across their backs
The ones that sought freedom NO MATTER what the cost
They toiled long and hard for you and me

Fought to keep their families together
Fought for some semblance of PEACE

Our Ancestors were not docile
They did resist slavery
They resisted "it" on the ship
They resisted "it" in the fields

How Beautiful.... how beautiful.

How Selfish are we The New Generation
So many of us do not acknowledge the hard work of our ancestors
We are not proud of the rich and diverse culture that composes the make up of you and I
Do we remember all that was done for us?
As we step into our 4 bedroom house with our 2 children and our luxury sedans parked in our 2.5 car garage....
Do we remember?

I fear that we have forgotten the blood of our
Ancestors that watered the Earth and brought forth...
LIFE
But we must not EVER forget the spirit and energy
that makes up our culture

We must not EVER forget the fact that we owe the
lives we live now to those that gave up their lives in
the past

It is time to acknowledge all parts of ourselves
Slowly time is slipping away from us
Grandmothers and Grandfathers are passing away
without anyone having a sense of their LEGACY

As the sun rises and sets on each new day, let us
reflect upon how different things could be
Let us give thanks to our Fathers and Mothers for
paving the way
Let us give back to our communities
Let us be as unselfish as our Ancestors were
Giving unselfishly because it's the right thing to do,
and not because we expect anything in return

From selfish to beautiful
You and I can surely learn to be...
Activists
Revolutionaries
Great Mothers and Fathers
Better Daughters and Sons

We owe that to our Ancestors.
We owe that to ourselves.

Old school
Brown culture

Inspiration

Being Black is about more than just slavery and the Civil Rights movement. It encompasses old stories and recipes passed down from one generation to another. It is about the transmission of history between grandparents and grandchildren. It is a story that should be told again and again so that it is never lost or forgotten.

Infinite Soul

This life is about so much more than possessions
It's about the connections that we make with one
another
It's about the legacy that we leave behind
That legacy is found in our mates and children
It's found in the precious memories that we have
created with others

We show people who we are by the way that we treat
them
        Not just by the words that we say
We show people our true character by the way that we
function in good times, and bad

I know right now that your physical body is not here,
but your Soul remains
And though I find it hard not to weep, I take solace in
the fact that this is NOT the end
I find joy in the fact that you were a Man of conviction
        A Man that was true to your word

**EVERYONE that has ever crossed your path felt the
LIGHT within you**

I am honored to have known you for this brief time
Honored that I had the chance to call you Friend

Yes, our time here is finite, but the lives that we

touch are Infinite
And while our earthly bodies may cease to exist, the
Heart, Spirit and Soul will last FOREVER

Inspiration

For anyone who has ever lost a loved one. [Dedicated to
Keith Ward. I know that you are resting in peace]

...On the Black-Hand Side

Give me 5 on the Black-Hand Side
And make it Real Legit
'Cause I'm lookin' for some good energy, no fakeness allowed
I'm lookin' for somebody that can relate to where I'm comin' from

We can sip Southern-style Sweet Tea
Play some Dominos
Talk mess about your Mama
Shoot....we can just sit still and reminisce about this thing called Life

Give me 5 on the Black-Hand Side
But don't you dare come 'round this piece talkin' bout how the "man" is holdin' you down
I ain't got NO TIME to hear that Mess

Just give me 5 on the Black-Hand Side

...And make sure that you bring over some of that
Cajun fried chicken
Greens (actually, I'd rather have Spinach)
Mashed Potatoes AND
Cornbread
Truthfully, we don't even have to eat
We can kick back and share knowledge
Discuss history and how we came to BE
Art
Philosophy
The Meaning behind the pyramids

We can debate MLK versus Muhammad versus Farrakhan
"Conversate" about the age-old mystery of whether Al's hair is relaxed or pressed

It's cool with me if you're not deep like that
I can be comfortable with silence, too
But I'd rather talk about something...
Better yet, I'd like to DO something

I'd rather do something to encourage young boys and girls to stay in school
Instead of depicting the Black family as sheer buffoonery, I'd prefer to see a more accurate portrayal of us in the media
I'd rather see a young man escorting elders to the bus stop, instead of robbing them
I'd rather hear about a pact between young Black women to attend Ivy League universities, instead of 6 best friends getting pregnant while still in high school

And you know what....
I take that back
I am NOT comfortable with silence, and you shouldn't be either

Give me 5 on the Black-Hand Side
But don't you dare SAY NOTHING
Don't you dare DO NOTHING

Give me 5 on the Black-Hand Side...and let's agree to work towards Change

Inspiration

A lot of people complain about social injustices, but they do not offer any tangible solutions. If you are concerned about the youth in your neighborhood, mentor one. Instead of grimacing in distaste when you see the homeless, volunteer at a local shelter or research alternative ways to get involved. The point is do not just sit idly by and do nothing.

Mantra

I LOVE my people.
I embrace and celebrate my culture.

Revolution

The revolution will not be televised
Loud speakers will not publicize that our people are
dying
Children having children –
Black men *and* women killing one another –
Whether by guns, drugs or unprotected sex, we are
killing our communities on a daily basis

Yes, it's true that the Revolution will NOT be televised

We as a People have a proud and storied history
From the rich red earth of Africa through the turmoil
and pain caused by slavery
We have seen and done much
So if all of this is true, when are we going to rise and
live up to the foundation that our ancestors have laid
for us?

When are we going to stop embracing stagnation and
move towards progress?
When are we going to stop talking about problems
and start coming up with solutions?
When are we going to stop laying stumbling blocks for
one another and start building each other up?

Complacency is definitely rampant
We are content to just coast by on the words "good
enough"
We are content because a Black president exists
We are content to do the minimum to survive
But is that really living?

In every family there is at least one that thinks
somebody owes them something
No one is owed anything

It is up to us to use our God-given intellect and talent
to make the world a better place for our great-great
grandchildren
It is up to us to make sure that our children know that
they are more than the color of their skin
They are more than the size of their house
They are more than the designer bag on their
shoulders and the Air Jordans on their feet
More than their ability to procreate

If we don't teach them to value themselves, who will?
If we don't teach them to love themselves, who will?
If we don't teach them that they are perfect and
wonderfully made because they were created by Our
Father, who will?

We have a responsibility to one another
That responsibility extends beyond
bloodlines...beyond neighborhoods...beyond
continents...
We have a responsibility to make each other the very
best that we can be
It is not a light responsibility, but it IS a necessary
responsibility

Because the simple truth of the matter is this —
The Revolution will NOT be televised
The Revolution is up to us
The Revolution is TODAY

The revolution is to be continued…

POWER & EQUALITY

Inspiration

The Black community has an amazing legacy of triumph and perseverance. Let's take care to preserve and extend that legacy with this and future generations.

Word is Bond?

When did we stop being a society that is based upon principles?
Why do people feel that it is perfectly acceptable to cheat and deceive?
What ever happened to loyalty and integrity?
What happened to respect regardless of viewpoint?

When did it become okay to break your word?

When did it become acceptable to break your bond?

Inspiration

I believe in the power of words and the impact of actions. Honor your word. Protect your bond. Speak and walk in your truth. Always be a man or woman of principle.

Bloodlines

Families share a special bond...a special connection...a special love
We are connected through the myriad of experiences that we share
Memories of birthday parties and Thanksgiving dinners...family feuds and the births of children
The shared pain of loss and the uplifting joy of accomplishments

Who else can be majorly pissed with you, but dare anyone else to say a word?
Who else can love you one second, and be ticked off with you the next?
Who else can tell from the sound of your voice whether you're having a rough day – even if you try to fake like everything is great?
Who else knows you inside out, and loves you anyway?

We are connected by the bond that unites us – a bond that is not necessarily dictated by blood
The connection is not always visible, but it's there
It's there in the way that a conversation is shared without speaking a word
It's there in the way that we catch each other when we fall
It's there no matter how far apart we are...

It is a connection that cannot be broken

Inspiration

The sense of belonging is so important! We all have a certain connection to our families, but in today's world, a "family" is not always about blood-ties. A family is anyone that you feel connected to through good and bad times...

Anyone that you can call on – regardless of whether it's convenient for them or not...

A family goes beyond bloodlines.

Love All Over Me

When you walk into the room, I feel a Connection
Shared Memories, Laughter, Tears
Moments in time that MEANT SOMETHING to Me
Precious Times that have helped to mold me into the
Woman that I am today

I want to hold on to those moments and create New
Treasures
Treasures that when we're 85 years old and not quite
as FLY, we can look back...
Look back, and always REMEMBER

Remember how we smiled and laughed into the rays
of the Sun
Feeling like that moment in time was Perfection
because we were with LOVED ONES
Concerts...Movies...Dinner Parties ...Road Trips
...Weddings...Babies...
So Many Precious Memories

I remember, too, Times when things were not so
bright...
The road was paved with tears and We held onto one
another like a port in a raging Storm
You Grounded me
Cemented me
You would NOT let me FALL
And I, in turn, would be your Rock when you needed
Support...
Someone that could LISTEN to your concerns, or
Speak up when you were not yet ready to walk in your

Truth

When you walk into the room, I feel and see
HISTORY....
Past, and in the making

You are my Friend...my FAMILY
There is a piece of You that I carry with me always

I know that Fate must have deigned it providence for
us to meet
Must have known that we would bring out the best
qualities in each other
That we would be accepting and understanding of one
another's faults

I do not worry that you will use my Weaknesses against
Me
I feel SAFE in your Presence
Secure in the sacred circle of TRUST that we have
created

Whenever our paths meet, I FEEL LOVE
It's all over me....all over you
There Is Love

Inspiration

There is something special about developing a deep bond with friends. I am talking about far more than the friend that you simply go to the movies with or that you only call when everything is going well. The type of friend I am talking about knows your deepest, darkest secrets – but does not judge you for them. The depth of friendship I'm referring to goes beyond the surface; he or she really SEES and loves you – flaws and all.

Mantra

I am appreciative for amazing friendships.
I will show myself to be a better friend
for nothing more than love's sake.

soulfree

back in the day it was ALL GOOD

i remember blue skies and endless days
honey-brown skin bathed by the warmth of the sun
hopscotch
tire swings
poppin now & laters and eatin sour pickles from The
Corner Candy Store

jumping rope
First Ten Speed Bike
roller skating
playing freeze tag and dodge ball
25 cent juice boxes with blue lips AND matching
tongue

First Crush
Sneaking Out to Meet Him and His Friends at the
Movies

wearing makeup to school hoping to NOT be caught
by my Mother -
telltale traces still visible ('cause it was cheap 99 cent
RED LIPSTICK)

Soul Flying
Not a Care in the World
I Thought That I'd Be Young Forever

Coming Into my Womanhood (at least, i thought so)...

big hoop earrings
ta-tas
first perm (silky smooth)
wearing my hair "down"

off-the-shoulder shirts
gossiping with my best friend about boys

homecoming games and rallies
school dances
feeling the beat of the music in my stomach
formal dresses
wearing my Mother's jewelry
feeling so grown-up

First REAL Date
My Hand Grasped in His
Butterfly Kisses
Heart Beating Fast

back in the day it was ALL GOOD

Soul Flying
Not a Care in the World
I Thought That I'd Be Young Forever

Inspiration

Back in the day it really was all good... Everything was SO SIMPLE. As a child, I had no concept of how good I had it!

Some things
never go out of style

G.A.W.

I am a Grown Ass Woman
I am not Defined by what you think of me
With or without your acceptance, I have ALWAYS been
a QUEEN

But you cannot grasp that knowledge because in so
many ways you are still a little girl playing dress up
You pretend to be wise and self-assured, BUT IN
REALITY you are a Colossal Mess
You are a bundle of insecurities and your lack of
confidence is apparent for all to see

Gossiping....trying to stir up actual interest in what
you have to say
Spitting venom to whatever sorry soul will pay you an
ounce of attention
CHILD, PLEASE....
All of that idle chitter chatter goes in one ear and
directly out the other

I remember wanting to have you believe in me
Like that somehow would justify all of the hard work
that I put in to BECOMING...

It took so long to discover my magnificence
So long to discover that joy is stitched into the soles of
my feet, and YES....
JOY...it leaps from my fingertips

You cannot steal my joy

See it FLOWS THROUGH MY VEINS like the River of Jordan
And it wraps itself around ALL those whom I hold dear

There is an inner peace that reverberates off the walls when I glide into the room
I do not have to demean people to garner attention
Because I AM.....a GROWN ASS WOMAN
Recognize, CHICK....and PLEASE stay in your lane

Inspiration

I recently came into contact with someone that I had not seen in years. Sometimes you encounter people that grow in grace and wisdom as they age; sometimes those people do not mature, but remain eternally "small".

Pimp Consolidation

Damn

Men don't even try to be creative anymore
Back in the day dudes would at least pretend that each
lady was special
I guess technology has changed ALL THAT

Bulk text messages to multiple women
Inboxing pictures of your "not-so-private-private"
parts
Poetic musings meant to inspire lust and drop panties

If you were really a true Pimp, you would just be Real

Please cease and desist with your tired lines and ploys
to get laid
Kick Rocks and Swallow Gravel, Playa
Your game is weak as hell and you have been found
out

Silly rabbit tricks are for kids, and we are well past
Good and Grown

I am not sure what understanding you have with your
other "friends"
But I am not interested in your shenanigans
Pimpin' ain't dead, but it sho nuff ain't being tolerated
over here

Inspiration

The opposite of a good man.

Black Girl

Hey there Black Girl.
Yes, I'm talking to you

Don't you think that you're somebody Special?
I mean, didn't anyone ever tell you that there is no one
like you
Every single hair strand, every inch of skin, every bone
in your body is unique and wonderfully made
Just. For. You.

You are so much more than the dip in your hips and the
curve of your thighs.

Your body is not for sale.
Your mind is not relegated to BET videos and hood
anthems
You are not limited to the perceptions of others

Black Girl, I am SO proud of you.
In spite of every obstacle that has been placed in your
way, you have succeeded spectacularly
You carry so much upon your shoulders, but you make
it look so simple

You are dynamic.
Keep going Black Girl
The stakes are high and it's too important for you to
stop now
Don't let anyone tell you that a Black Girl cannot make
it to the top
Keep pushing...keep pushing...keep pushing...

Who knows how many future generations are
dependent upon the decisions that you make today?

Be guided by love, principles and peace.
If all of your decisions are based upon these solid
cornerstones, you cannot go wrong
But most of all Black Girl – BELIEVE IN YOURSELF
Define what success is for You

You are unstoppable.

I should know
I AM a Black Girl.

Inspiration

As a woman of color, sometimes it is really difficult to get past all of the walls that are erected around us. We are battling age-old perceptions of **Who** we are and **What** we represent. Then add onto those layers the pressure and expectations that we place upon ourselves. This poem is really a representation of what I want for ALL girls {women} — I have placed special significance on Black girls because I feel that they face additional pressures. I want them (especially the younger generation) to know that regardless of what their past contains, they are conquerors. They can do and be anything that they put their mind to.

Thickness

There is power in this Body
Power beyond the caramel brown skin that covers
All This Goodness

I used to be caught up in the physical
Never quite satisfied with the attributes that I was
gifted
>...warm chocolate eyes
>...generous breasts
>...a smile that rivals the sun

I remember lamenting about how I wished my legs
were long and lean, *but*
Look How Far *These* Legs Have Allowed Me To Go
>They have taken me farther than even I knew I
>could go...

Yes, there is so much Power in *this Body*
>Creative Energy
>Depth of Character
>Someone who has fallen, but made the
>decision not to stay down
>Someone who has decided that she is *worthy*
>of every good thing life has to offer

On some days I still struggle with the physical...
But I now realize what a marvelous gift *this body is*

It's a shame that society teaches us to emulate others,
instead of embracing ourselves

Do you realize how much power exists within You?

Inspiration

There is so much power within each one of us waiting to be acknowledged and put into action!

Mantra

I Embrace this Skin.
I Love this Body.
I Celebrate EVERYTHING about me.

EMBRACE
the skin you're in…

III

BitterSweet

Jonesin
Found
Girlfriend
Subtext
Life college degree
Love's Kiss
Tú
Gone
Mate Forgiveness Worthy
Soldier
Ready Transparency Attraction
Questions
Unbreakable boy
Everything
Opened
Soul Love
Poetry Feeling
Recuerda
Sidechick Judas
Clean
Bitter Sweet
Wounds
Hustle
Besos Slate Way
Storms
Kisses

"I love you without knowing how, or when, or from where. I love you simply, without problems or pride: I love you in this way because I do not know any other way of loving but this, in which there is no I or you, so intimate that your hand upon my chest is my hand, so intimate that when I fall asleep your eyes close."

(Pablo Neruda)

*I*s there any emotion more complex or confusing than love? In the beginning, it's all shiny and new. There are sublime feelings of euphoria, hope and spine-tingling excitement. Later when the shininess wears off, there are still moments of bliss; they are just intermingled and oftentimes weighed down by "outside issues" (trust, pride, financial matters, etc.).

BitterSWEET is a beautiful story of love, loss, passion and ultimately, redemption.

Subtext

You speak words to me
Words that abound with imagery
Words that make me imagine...what if...what if you
and I became WE...
Words that wrap me up in pink cashmere dreams and
float me on clouds of splendor
We talk about life...the past...the future
We talk about everything and nothing
Yet you speak words to me
Words that make me imagine...what if...what if you
and I became WE

Inspiration

Quite simply....HIM.

Feeling You

I am really into you, boy.

I like the way that you move
And the way that you speak
And the way that you interact with others

I like the way that I feel when I'm around you.

I enjoy your quiet confidence
The way that you articulate your thoughts
I LOVE the way that you say my name

Are you into me too?

I'm a little bit shy, so if you are I need for you to give
me a sign
'Cause I really (really, really) want to make you mine

This is an advance notice that I want to be Your Girl.

Inspiration

The first stirrings of attraction.

Attraction

My heart beats for you
Like the staccato rhythm of raindrops against a
windowpane, it beats strong and steady
It speeds up at just the mention of your name

I wish that I could find the words to express how you
make me feel
Like fireflies dance around the night sky, I am drawn to
you
It's almost like I'm helpless to respond

Inspiration

Attraction — plain, but not always simple.

college boy.

i see u and tremble
u don't even notice.

i feel your presence like cool rain on warm skin
yet you remain oblivious.

i am inspired by u
moved by u
touched by u
u don't even realize it.

the thrill of u is overwhelming
for u see, i am in love with your mind
and my heart beats only for u.

Inspiration

This poem is a sentimental favorite. When I was a
student at the University of Illinois, I met this amazing
writer. I would sit and listen to him, and I just felt so
inspired. Actually, he inspired me to write my earliest
poems at the Illini Union in Champaign, IL - - - the rest
is history.

Sidechick Hustle

You can gon' ahead with all of that madness
Talkin' bout "have I found my Prince Charming"
And can you be my "Mr.-In-The-Meantime"

Do not project your alley cat mentality and morals
upon me

I do not need or want your drama and duplicity
My life is full, and quite frankly I am not interested in a
starring role as your Sidepiece

You can gon' ahead with all of that foolishness
Telling me all the things you THINK I want to hear

What I truly desire is sincerity
A man of substance
Someone who can call me anytime, not just when the
coast is clear

I tell you that I enjoy your friendship
You tell me that you want to be more than just my
friend

I tell you that I like our conversations
You respond with how much you love me...
Riiiight...you want to "love" me right up out of my
clothes
Want to love me out of all my treasures – treasures
that you have no right to
Treasures that you are totally undeserving of

I want a holistic Connection

You only want to connect with Twin Peaks and Booty
Cheeks

Sorry sweetie, but I am not interested in your
headboard games
My mental capabilities are fully functioning, and for
you there is a NO VACANCY sign in place

I honestly do not understand some men

Why would you think that I would want to dishonor
another woman's relationship in that manner?
...Dishonor myself?

My mind, heart, body and soul are sacred to me
And no part of me wants any entanglements or Soul
Ties with you

Baby, I'm not tryin' to hear NONE of your Sidechick
hustle
I've heard about three years too many of your inane
chatter already
Three years of your quest to be granted a piece of
something that you can never have
You cannot comprehend, let alone value the Majesty
of ME

And while I appreciate your newfound honesty, I have
no desire to be complicit in your games
I ain't got NO desire to be your honeydip...girl on the
side piece...chick that you just want to FLIP
Naw man....I ain't tryin' to hear no more of your
Sidechick Hustle

Inspiration

About 4 years ago I met this man who was very smooth, easy to talk to and attractive. When we met I was attracted to him and he was attracted to me, but's that all it ever was. We really did not talk about anything of real substance and I never really pressed for us to be on that type of level. He and I were just "cool". The truth is, even in the beginning I knew that he and I were not well suited.

At some point during our friendship he became involved in a long-term relationship. When he would call it was always from work or while he was on the road. If I called him and he was at home, he would not answer the phone. Finally one day he asked me "have you found your Prince Charming"? When I said no, he went on to basically ask if he could be my friend with benefits. Wow! That was the beginning of the end of our friendship – if in fact we were ever truly friends. I do understand that in today's society, many people do not have a problem with being someone's mistress. Personally, I desire to have my own partner, not sneak around with someone else's! A cautionary word to the sidepiece: If you are waiting to be a woman of importance in his life, that is likely <u>NEVER</u> going to happen. He has already shown you what you are worth to him.

Questions (If I Was Your Girlfriend)

If I Was Your Girlfriend would you Love, Honor and
Cherish Me?
...Be honest with me, even if you knew that it could
potentially
hurt Me...hurt Us

Would you Trust me with your deepest fears,
desires...your Essence?
...Those Light and Dark parts of yourself?

Would you open your Heart to me?
Believe that I would NEVER use your weaknesses
against You?

Would you RESPECT ME?
Respect me enough to Communicate your
Needs...your Wants...your Everything?

If I Was Your Girlfriend, I would Honor You
I would support you as you pursue your dreams
I would accept you as the Man that you are
...Not attempt to Mold you into who I want you to be

Like the petals of a rose, I would enfold you in my Love
Guard your Heart with my Heart
Love you through all continuums of Joy and Pain

I would willingly accept you and whatever baggage
that entails
When you fall, I would carry you while you gather your
Strength

If I Was Your Girlfriend I Would LOVE YOU
Your Intellect...Talents... Character
Flaws...Strengths...Weaknesses
    I Would Love You

Can you love me that completely?
I'm asking you...
Can you love ME that completely?

Inspiration

A relationship is about more than just taking – it takes trust, honesty, communication and a plethora of other things to make a relationship go the distance. A lot of people are good at taking, but for a relationship to work you need to be willing to give, too.

Besos (Kisses)

Your mouth is Soft like the petals of a new blossom
Kisses gentle.
Your embrace is Strong like the oldest of oak tress
Comforting embrace.
You rain kisses down upon me and it feels like...
BLISS.

Inspiration

The intimacy of a kiss – especially when it's with the right person.

He Wants My...Poetry

He doesn't think I realize it, but I KNOW
I KNOW he wants my...POETRY

Wants me to Give him Everything, while I receive
Nothing but feelings of Emptiness
He sends me lyrical expressions of lust
All in the interest of unlocking my verbal trousseau

He is slick with the use of his Words
Spinning webs of poetic fancy
Seeking to draw me in closer...

But I am not fooled because I KNOW he just wants my
POETRY

Wants to evoke emotional and sentimental responses
so that I Yield
Intertwined with his notes, words and phrases until I
melt away
Tangled up in his web of articulate seduction

But I cannot give in
I love myself too much to give in to his romantic
schemes

See, my Poetry is special
It is a gift that is meant to be shared with a King, not a
slick-talking Jester

I confess that a part of me does wish that he were sincere
But the Wise Woman in me already KNOWS

I KNOW that he just wants my POETRY

Inspiration

One day I was having a discussion with my good friends about a new dating interest. For months this person had pursued me, and finally I agreed to go out with him. I told my friends that I was skeptical of his genuine interest and felt that he was merely after my poetry. They both laughed and said only if my "poetry" was a metaphor for something else.

Transparency

I just want you to SEE me
To see all of the elements that make me special

I am so much more than this SKIN
All of these molecules and atoms are fused together and in
their totality they form my body
BUT, I am more than just this body

I am an imperfect being, but I was wonderfully and
perfectly made

I have big dreams, aspirations and desires
I expect A LOT from myself
Really, I expect nothing short of Greatness

Yet somehow, I sense that you don't grasp that

I constantly feel like you just tell me things that you think I
want to hear
The truth is I could do without your empty sentiments
I am not impressed by your hollow platitudes

I really just want you to SEE me
To honor the flawlessness that exists within my
Imperfections
To totally get all of the little quirks that make me, ME
To recognize the Depth of Character that resides within this
Shell

I Just Want You To See Me

Inspiration

I was dating someone new and it felt like every other sentence involved comments about sex. I do get that interest in sex is normal, but I wanted him to see me beyond the physical. I really wanted to connect in a deep and intense way - moreso on an emotional/metaphysical-type level. We were not looking for the same things, and it did not take long for me to realize that not only could we not have a relationship; we did not even have enough of a foundation to be friends.

So Worthy

I guess somebody didn't tell you how magnificent I am
How I'm loved beyond measure
That I am worth more than money, jewels...any
material possession you can think of

Someone neglected to pass along the PSA that I am
SPECTACULAR
That I am filled with Joy, and represent Grace,
Empowerment and Love

You didn't get the message, did you?

Why else would you think that I would hang around
waiting for you?
Why else would you think we could pick up where we
left off in this fictional relationship?

How can I return to being your Girl when you were
most definitely never My Man?

After all of this time you are still incredibly selfish
You still think that the world revolves around your
needs and wants

Since our time together I have *Transcended*
Now more than ever I recognize the Power that lies
within me

I know what I deserve
I know what I want
I know that I am Worthy

I am Worthy to be showered with Sincere love and appreciation
To be courted with more than mere words and empty moments in time
To be with a Man who knows who he is and what he wants

You say that you're ready to be my Man
Are you?
Are you really a man?

The truth is I doubt that you know what a Real Man is

A real man does not run
A real man is able to admit past mistakes

I'm not angry with you...I'm really not
It's just that I have moved beyond
I have moved Beyond whatever it is we had

You experienced the Splendor of me and you let it go

Inspiration

A good friend of mine dated this guy for a period of time and out of nowhere he disappeared. About a year later he resurfaced expecting to continue where they left off... Needless to say, he was given his permanent walking papers!

Jonesin'

You are deeply ingrained in my soul like bass notes
meet hip-hop joints
I'm talkin' all I do is think about you
How can we be together and ride out until sun meets
set

So what, so what, so what's the scenario?
I'm checkin', checkin', checkin' for the scenario
Trying to get to know your kinfolks, your frat brothers
AND all your childhood friends
Memories of shared laughter, walks together hip to
hip, summertime house parties AND
hands joined in prayer

I feel like our lives are interwoven
You are so good to me
When my days are long you make me smile
You love all of my worries and past hurts away

I have never known anyone like you
I feel at complete ease in your company...like I can be
myself at all times

You are such a GOOD MAN
I just want to be a better woman for myself and You

You are inside my heart like words and poetry
Like a track on repeat, I cannot get you off my mind

The purity of your Soul knocks me off my feet

Baby, I carry your heart with me ALWAYS
I love everything about you
More than the words that consume my whole being, I
love you

Everything about you is so beautiful to me
You Set My Soul Free

Inspiration

Love.

I Found Love

From the moment that we met, I knew that I would
love you
I remember the sparkle of curiosity and interest in your
eyes
I was excited by the possibility of what might come to
exist between us
In truth, I was intrigued by you

We would talk for hours at a time about anything and
everything – no topic was off limits
We never seemed to run out of things to discuss
We never seemed to tire of one another

You burned like a fire deep in my soul
And like a moth to a flame, I needed to be close to you

I wanted to hear your hopes and dreams
I wanted desperately to be a part of your future

Do you remember those times?

I was drowning in the sea of love, but did not want to
be saved
Not as long as we were in the waves together

I remember the exact moment when I fell in love with
you

Inspiration

The beginning of "new" love.

Gone

I felt you slipping away from me
Like smooth silk in clumsy hands
Your eyes no longer clear with sparkling joy to see me
Our connection
Broken

I knew that there was a change, but I was powerless
to stop it
I wanted to tell you how much you meant to me...how
deeply I loved you
But in the end, I just watched you fade away

I thought that magically you would come back to me
That somehow we could be one again
But we never resurfaced

In the end, I just watched you fade away

I never wanted to let you go
I never meant to let you go

Inspiration

The departure of love's embrace.

Judas Kiss

Hands intertwined
Dark espresso eyes
connected with mine...slowly pulling me in
Your kiss is
...Seductive
It offers promises that cannot possibly be kept

For the first time in a long time I want to believe

I would like nothing more than to
Submit
To paint abstract scenes that juxtapose until we are
Mentally connected
Racing to trace arcs where you Start and I Begin and
we Meet in the Middle

Your Kiss is
Seductive
Offering Promises that Cannot be Kept

Yet Still, I Want To Believe

My heart is in need of resuscitation
Bruised from before...in search of *SOMETHING*
but
In the deepest recesses of Self, I recognize that you are
the Ultimate Deceiver
I am Light and you want to swallow me whole
Devour my sweetness...Drink in my Soul...Steal My
Fire
To you, I am insignificant...just a Physical means to an

end dressed up in Meaningless Words

The Words...the Words don't MATTER to you
But Words always matter to me
There is POWER in WORDS
Boundless Energy
So Much Power

I refuse to be dragged into your silk-lined tapestry of deceit
Wrapped in nothing but your empty sentiments

...But the memory of your kiss is
SEDUCTIVE
Worse, it has Awakened a Sleeping Memory
The Desire to Be One Part of a Whole

A part of me wishes that we had never met...
The Judas was in your Kiss

Inspiration

Sometimes we meet people that are disingenuous. We have to listen to that inner voice that is usually spot-on. If we don't listen and later on we are hurt, we really have no one to blame but ourselves.

My Soul Opened Up

I wish that I had known myself the way that I needed
to.
       Treasured myself
       Seen the God within myself

If I had known what I needed to know, I would not
have held on...
       ...So Long
       ...So Hard
       ...So Needlessly

I would not have placed my Heart in your hands
Would not have spent so much Time thirsting for your
love
I would not have granted you so much Power

The Wisdom in me would have seen the Child in you
       Would have known that you were consumed
       by thoughts of "I", "Me", "Mine"
Selfish.
Self-Important.
Materialistic.
       Thoughts of only Self.

The essence of me wanted to be there for what I
perceived to be the king in you

But it was all a vagary of imagination
You were a whisper-thin shadow, and not at all the
man of substance I thought you to be

Still, it is difficult to express in words or verbalize the emotions behind how I felt...
For the longest time I felt like my heart was being ripped to shreds
Milliseconds, Days, Months, Years...Infinity
What seems like an absolute lifetime spent loving you with every Molecule of my Being

I created this visage of a man that I thought existed, but that person was never real.

Until finally through space, time and destiny my Soul just opened up
...My Soul opened up and the pearl of Truth was Revealed
Truth walked in, settled on my lap and had a PERSONAL CONVERSATION with me
It was like Magic...
All of a sudden it became crystal clear that my love had been wasted on you...
You did not deserve it
In actuality, you NEVER deserved it

One day my Soul opened up...
And my heart was finally free.

Inspiration

Love is a precious gift and there is absolutely nothing wrong with loving someone. The mistake is not in taking the risk to love, but in languishing in feelings of misery and rejection if the love is not returned. I really loved this man with every molecule of my being. In fact, I spent so much time loving him that I never realized that I had created a larger than life person who did not exist.

Allow yourself the time to grieve over the fact that your love was not returned in the way that you needed it to be returned, and then move on. You can never hope to have the love that you seek if you are immersed in a person that does not feel the same way about you. Somewhere out there exists a person who is capable of loving you the way that you DESERVE to be loved.

Mantra

I believe that I am WORTHY of love.

Real love

is not always smooth

Recuerdo Tú

Recuerdo el momento
Cuando estuvimos juntos baja la luna

Me acuerdo tú cara
            Los manos
La boca
            Tús besos

Me acuerdo de ti

Translation:

I remember the moment
When we were together under the moon

I remember your face
            Your hands
Your mouth
            Your kisses

I remember you

Inspiration

...I think that I'll keep that one for myself...

Everything

You were my everything
For as long as I can remember, I loved you and only you
I loved the way that your mind worked
I thought that you were so clever and generous
Full of creativity and talent

In my heart I felt that our destinies were forever
intertwined
That nothing and no one could ever come between us
I never sensed that there would be an end to us

Was I not smart enough...pretty enough...thin
enough...successful enough?

Ultimately the answer really does not matter
Because even with all that you have done to me, I still
miss you
I miss our four-hour long conversations about
everything and nothing all at the same time
I miss your offbeat sense of humor
I miss existing in the same space as you
I miss the person that I thought I knew

I guess a part of me still loves you
I still want to hear your hopes and dreams
I still want to reach for heaven's delight for you

Will I always measure every man against you?
I am afraid that the memory of my love for you will
haunt me forever

Inspiration

My first love... It's weird how you can build someone up
to be this larger than life person. For better or worse, I
have never loved anyone with the purity of heart that I
loved him. He is the only man that I have ever loved
unconditionally. In truth, he is the only man I have ever
allowed myself to love.

Some relationships leave a mark that lasts forever...

Unbreakable

Sometimes I wish that we could go
Back

Once upon a time we were Friends
We shared secrets
Between us there was
History

Little by little I fell in Love with you
I NEVER meant for that to happen
Had no clue that it would forever change the
Framework of us

Still...we were
Connected

Talking for hours about Nothing and Everything
When I really needed a Confidante, you were there
I felt safe with you
Comfortable with sharing my Hopes and
Fears

I wanted nothing but the Best for You

Your engagement hit me like a Tsunami
Wasn't this the same man that said he did not want to
be Married?

Still...we were Connected...just in a
Different Way

I listened to your concerns...all of your Worries
I was there for you to share your burdens

In the end I was the Ultimate Friend to you

I only wish that I could say the same about you...
You Drifted Away
You Lied and said that you looked for me...that you
called
But it was just that...A LIE
Everything About You Was A Lie

For so long the thought of you made me
Cold
No More Warmth
No More Joy At The Mention Of Your Name
just an empty feeling at how you used my love to your
advantage

I don't feel that way anymore, though...
There are no regrets that I Loved You
No second-guessing the fact that I hurt myself, rather
than hurt you

I thought that we were Unbreakable...
That our Bond would stand the test of time

How could the person that I loved be so Selfish?

Inspiration

The heart wants what the heart wants, right? For so
many years I felt like he was meant to be my Soul Mate.
Now I'm not sure if such a thing exists... The romantic
part of me certainly would like to think so. What I do
know is this – friendship is to be honored at ALL TIMES.
When it's not, you have to walk away.

Storms

We have now come to the point where a parting of
ways is inevitable
For so many years of my life I have given you passion,
soul and commitment
We have had some sweet moments, but more and
more storm clouds have threatened our once peaceful
coexistence

With each passing year I care a little less
I work harder and harder to feel connected to you, but
something is missing
At times I feel almost nothing
Your softness has faded away

I have to leave you now my friend, before the flames
of my passion turn to disdain

I would like to leave you with warm honeyed thoughts
and words of wisdom
But I really don't have much left to say
I really did love you, but now it's time to say goodbye

Inspiration

Do not put your time or energy into people, organizations, relationships, [insert whatever term applies to you here], that are not mutually satisfying and beneficial (and no, that's not selfish). I am telling you from experience that sometimes people are opportunistic and self-serving, and will use you until they use you up (and have no qualms about doing so). In the end I had to let go of this particular relationship. [For **Bernadette J. Carroll,** who in 2003 spoke the following words to me, and I have *__never__* forgotten them: "Because I love myself, I will not allow others to disrespect me."] Live life by this principle, and you will not regret it.

Mantra

I respect myself and
will not tolerate any less
from those around me.

Love's Soldier

I thought I'd lost the use of my heart
It was so wrapped up in thoughts of You...I....We
So consumed by wanting to be with you in any way
possible
I was crestfallen when I realized that it was a DREAM
Devastated that the poet of my heart was a mere
illusion

Before I knew what true Love was, there was you
I loved you with all of my Heart, Mind and Soul
Drifted through cotton candy and bliss-filled dreams
where we existed as One

Mentally, you captivated me
I never tired of your voice, your imagination, the way
that you linked thoughts together
It was like electrons, neutrons and synapses all fired
on full power
I tried to resist, but the truth is I loved EVERYTHING
ABOUT YOU
Beyond that, I Trusted You
I trusted you with my hopes, dreams and deepest
fears

I don't know why I wasted so much time...why I put so
much of myself into Loving you
I wished for you the Moon and Stars, and you left me
with Desert Sands
I Protected your Feelings (even to the peril of my own)
I Treasured your Heart (and you Trampled Mine)
Left me as a Muddled, Confused Mess
Seemingly incapable of loving anyone else

Left in a prison of my own design...my love for you
still lingering in my mind

But I'm a Soldier of Love
Pressing forward, patiently waiting for the One that
will TREASURE my Heart
See the miraculous Beauty in all of my imperfections

I will not hide from him any longer
I will no longer seek comfort in the shadows
You left me with grains of sand, and now a rare
PEARL has emerged

I know that Love will come
I salute and surrender myself to Love's Embrace

Cover Me
Fold me into Your arms
Come and Find Me
Make Me Yours

Inspiration

Moving on from an old love.

I'm Ready

For the longest time I have shielded myself from others
The emotions that are deepest to my heart have been kept hidden
But no more

I'm ready

I'm ready to give 100% to that special someone
I'm ready to be everything that he needs and more

I'm ready to be his soul mate
His helpmate
His lover and his friend

I'm willing to be his confidante
His partner
I'm willing to be there through the good and bad times

God has been preparing me for him all of my life

I'm ready to be patient and kind
To be the arms that embrace and comfort him when he's had a rough day
I am ready to love all of his hurt and pain away

To treat his perfections and imperfections equally
I am ready to accept him for who he is, without trying to mold him into who I want him to be

I want to be there to support him through every triumph and fall
I am ready to pray for him when he does not have the strength to pray for himself

I am ready for love

Inspiration

I am opening my heart to the possibility of love.

Soul Mate

My beloved, I am waiting patiently for you
I know that you exist and I will not lose Faith
Did you know that I dream about you?
It's true

I dream about the day that I give my heart to you
Dream about the life that we'll build together
The memories that will unfold in glorious splendor
The creation of our Family
Growing old with you

I cannot wait to meet you.

I know that every experience has been meant to
Prepare me for you
You are going to be the King of my Heart, and I the
Queen of yours
Together we are going to achieve great things
Love each other through every circumstance
Reach further than we might have, because we will be
there to catch one another when we fall

I know that times won't always be easy
I am not perfect and I know that you are not either
But I still Love you
I still want every good and perfect thing for you
I long to make you smile

I desire a life with you
Life with all of its nuances of joy and pain is still
preferable to a life without you

Together we will circumnavigate and transcend mind and soul
Our affirmation of love is going to be renewed daily
In this battle of love, we will each make fist and fight to stay Together

You don't know it yet, but you are my Soul Mate.
Baby, you're my Soul Mate.

Inspiration

My future soul mate.

Infinity (to the nth degree)

I want to be with you 4ever
Paint the sky with millions of stars that attest to my
love for you
I love you unwaveringly
There is not a nanosecond when I do not Love You
You make me feel like I was Created to be with you
Created to love you for all time

You are a Treasure to behold
Sometimes I want to steal away to another place that
is far away
A place that is reserved for just you and I

Hold onto me
Through the fires of uncertainty and the darkness that
paints the night
Hold onto me

You fill my life with so much color and vitality
The Light in you beckons to the core of me
I want to be a better Woman for you
Lay the moon, galaxy and the Heavens at your feet
Fill your heart with Joy, Peace and Happiness, and so
much LOVE
So much Love that your Being glows with the POWER
of it

Melt with me
Let your Soul become entangled with my Soul until
we are 1
United, but two distinct entities that have willingly

chosen the Bliss of becoming One

Like a moth to a flame, you have CAPTURED me
I want to be with you and Only You
Everything within me is yours
Everything WITHIN ME is yours
EVERYTHING within me is YOURS

Inspiration

Him.... I *know* that he's out there.

The Love of My Life

You take me to mountaintops and valleys that I never
knew existed
Your sweet melody is like a burst of sunshine on a
cloudy day
With you, I feel like I am drifting on feelings of sheer
bliss
You touch me in ways that I just cannot explain

You take me higher than I have ever known

I wait for you to speak to me
And you do...
You pull me into your web until I am helpless to
respond

You sweep me away on tidal waves of emotion
I am wrapped up in your song and you will not let me
go

You are like the greatest of mysteries and the closest
of friends
I confide all of my heart and soul to you and you
welcome it
I offer up my inner turmoil and angst and you accept
those feelings, too

You thrill and excite me
Sometimes you beckon to me in the still of night
Visions of notes, words and harmonies flash across the
landscape of my imagination
They dance through my veins and consume me

I love the way that you make me feel
You and you alone understand the intensity and
depth of my passion

You are my love
You are my sweet relief
You are MUSIC

Inspiration

This is probably one of my favorite poems! Perhaps
your music may be a man or woman...or your faith.
Whatever your "music" is, doesn't it take you to
heights that you never knew existed?

Music...such sweet relief

Wounds in the Way

There is so much that I want to share with you
So many thoughts
So many feelings
So many emotions

But every time my lips part to say the words
The wounds get in the way

I want to tell you how deeply you hurt me
I want to tell you how part of me feels like it's missing
without you
I want to tell you that even though I love you – things
can never be the same
I want to tell you that words are precious, and once
stated, a mountain of apologies cannot change what
was said

I want to tell you this...and so much more
But my pride, and yes the wounds
The wounds get in the way

Inspiration

I am not a person that enjoys sharing my emotions.
Sometimes, though, if you are hurting badly enough,
you just have to find a way to get through the pain. I
remember praying and crying at the same time. The
wounds are still in the way, but maybe someday they
won't be...

Forgiveness

Memories resurface
I am often reminded of a simpler time
A time when I depended upon and trusted you
A time when we laughed, talked and confided

But that was before
Before your words and actions changed everything
Before my experience with you changed how I relate
to the people in my life

I am trying really hard to forgive you because I know
that's the right thing to do
But it's difficult...

The phantom of hurt dances across my memory at
inopportune moments
At times I am happy to see you
At times the mere sight of you disgusts me

You are an Ice Queen
Seemingly incapable of understanding how much you
hurt me

It is hard to move past the memory of tears that skate
between you and I

Still, slowly I am moving in the right direction
I smile a bit more when our paths meet and grit my

teeth a lot less
My spirit feels lighter
Finally my heart feels open to the possibility...

Forgiveness is definitely not an easy process

Inspiration

The process of forgiving someone can be so complicated. Why is it that when people hurt you the most, it seems like they don't realize it (or realize it and don't care)? Hurt feelings definitely exist beyond romantic relationships – even life-long friends can sometimes hurt you. Forgiveness is difficult, but the inability to forgive leads to bitterness. Everyone makes mistakes; make it a habit to forgive other people *and yourself.*

Clean Slate

Forgiveness is Cleansing
It renews the Spirit
Makes all things New
           The Heart Feels Lighter

Inspiration

Letting go of old hurts, disappointments and anger is SO FREEING. The old adage says that forgiveness is not just for the other person; it's for us too. Holding on to past hurts and disappointments weighs us down, and it takes up so much energy. If you are still holding on to old pain from 11.5 years ago (or even from last week), let it go! I promise that you will feel better.

Mantra

I believe in forgiveness for myself and others.
I will not cling to old wounds,
hurts and disappointments.

IV
Unlimited Possibilities

Metamorphosis
Mountaintop
POSSIBILITIES
Univer SOUL
Exclusively
Baggage
Dance
TruthFly
PHAT
Unlimited
Faithful
UNLIMITED
Inspired
Transcendence
Freedom
Side
Golden
Beauty

"Think of the world you carry within you."

(Rainer Maria Rilke)

So much potential exists within each one of us. There is potential to change not just ourselves, but those around us. Bad things do occur – that is just a fact of life. Do you know the differentiating factor in separating a positive experience from a negative experience...a good relationship from a bad relationship...even joy versus pain? It's merely in the way that you CHOOSE to handle the situation...how you choose to process the information. There is VALUE in every situation – whether good or "bad".

Within each one of us there is a kernel of greatness. There is truly NOTHING that you cannot accomplish... NOTHING that you cannot overcome. Believe in yourself – believe in the possibilities. **Unlimited Possibilities is a love letter to myself and YOU.**

Transcendence

I knew that I could do it
Fly amongst the clouds
Be one with the Universe and Myself

I knew that if I could just rise above the ordinary
If I could reach within myself and find that needle-
head of greatness, that I would...
EVOLVE

If I could get out of my own way
Listen and be respectful of others' opinions, but not
care what they think
Trust myself
Trust my instincts

I knew that I could do it
I could take ownership of my life
Tear down the walls of doubt and fear
Build a monument of grace and empowerment

I knew that I could DO IT

I could be the Woman that the Creator always
intended -
Confident and Poised
Forgiving and Kind
Proud of my accomplishments AND failures
Accepting of my shortcomings

Accepting of my humanity

Finally I have moved beyond self...beyond
situation...beyond circumstance
I recognize that I am more than the fear of failure that
sometimes threatens to swallow me whole
I am more than any problem or stumbling block
*Nothing and no one can stop me from achieving my
Destiny*

I knew that I could ASCEND
Walk with my head held high and proudly proclaim
that I have arrived
Like a Phoenix from the ashes, I too rose again
I, too, am experiencing a rebirth
I, too, am MAGNIFICENT

RADIANT
Like a thousand beams of light, I feel RADIANT

I feel it
I know that my Light is shining for the entire world to
see
I realize that this Life is a beautiful and wonderful
GIFT, and I will treat it as such
I will cherish each day that is granted to me with a
heart full of thankfulness and joy

I will continue to grow...learn...experience
I will continue to evolve....to transform

Continue to ascend

My journey is not complete...
I want to be all that I am capable to be

Inspiration

The beginning of recognizing my PURPOSE.

There is tremendous value in solitude and reflection

So Fly

I just want to Fly

I mean like the boldest eagle in the bluest sky
I want to Fly
Fly beyond all of the expectations others have of me
Beyond all of the limitations that I have placed on
myself

I just want to dance
To boldly leap from scene to scene
Capturing the intensity and magic of each moment
Light-hearted
Joyful
Happy
Dancing to a rhythm beating slowly and surely in my
head
It is a beat that is only for my ears to hear
It is a rhythm that is only for my heart to *feel*

I just want to sing
I mean like Ella Fitzgerald or Leontyne Price
Bold
Strong
Proud
I want to sing until the Heavens burst
Until nightingales marvel at my song

I just want to live
To live the best life I can live
To live life with no regrets

I just want to BE
To be at true peace with myself and the decisions that I make
To be the Woman I know that I was meant to be
To do the Great Things I know that God wants me to do

I just want to SOAR
Higher than the constellations and stars that I view at night
Higher than even I knew I could go

Beautifully
Inexplicably
Awesomely
I am transcending beyond Self
I am Calm
I am at Peace
I am Me
And that's all I ever needed to be

Inspiration

Be comfortable with who you are and what you represent; everything else will fall into place.

Exclusively

I am loving you
EXCLUSIVELY
'Cause you fill me with so much JOY
Joy like the first rays of spring sunshine
Like when the flowers surround me with their sweet
fragrance
So much Joy that I can hardly put it into words

Yes, I am loving you
EXCLUSIVELY

I feel at peace when I am in your company
I enjoy our private conversations
I feel secure in your love

I think I may have taken you for granted before
But not anymore...

'Cause I am loving YOU
EXCLUSIVELY

Giving you the time that you are so deserving of
Rejoicing in the tidbits of information that I glean from
you each day
The cleverness...
The playfulness...
The shyness that sometimes is bolstered by a burst of
boldness...
The sheer delight that is YOU

I am LOVING YOU...

EXCLUSIVELY

Spiritually and Mentally
Physically and Psychologically
Holistically
I am embracing EVERYTHING about you

From the crown of your head, to the soles of your feet
I am loving you EXCLUSIVELY
For you see, you and I are One
We are twins, and the mirror image of you reflects the
core of ME

Yes, you heard right
I am LOVING ME...
EXCLUSIVELY

Inspiration

It took so long to discover the power of ME. For many
years I put the wants and needs of others before myself.
I did not fully grasp that I mattered, too. **You have to
love yourself and know your self-worth before you
can completely love someone else.**

true love begins within

Me.

Just when I thought all was lost, I found love
I rediscovered a zest for life that I thought was gone
Each day became more and more meaningful
I began to thank God for ALL things – big and small
The ability to breathe...to listen...to feel
The ability to think and reason – for the gift of a sound
mind – for the gift of peace of mind

Just when I'd sunk into a bottomless pit of despair, I
resurfaced...
I found an inner strength that I'd forgotten I possessed
Strength in the character that was instilled in me by
my Mother
Strength in my beliefs...my convictions
Strength in my ability

Just when I had begun to think that I couldn't make it, I
found JOY
The kind of joy that made me want to shout from the
mountaintops that I'd arrived
The kind of joy that made me feel like anything was
possible

Just when I had begun to question everything – even
who I was
I found something powerful and wonderful
Something amazing that can never be recreated
because it's the only one of its kind
Just when I thought I'd lost it all, God picked me up and
I FOUND ME

Inspiration

I reached a point where it seemed like nothing was going well. I was trying my best, but still I kept hitting brick halls. With each successive failure, my will to fight lessened. I was literally a shell of the vibrant and confident person that I knew. Then slowly, things started to fall into place. With each step forward I became more certain that I was headed in the right direction. I just had to get knocked around a bit to know that I can handle anything that life throws my way (**and believe me if you are going through a difficult time, You Can Make It, Too**). All that is required is **<u>FAITH</u>**!!!

Mantra

I believe in the power of ME.

Inspired: Golden

I am living my life like it's Golden
I put out the vibes that I want to receive back

When everything is said and done, I want to be
known for being a
Real Woman
A Woman of Grace, Distinction and Empathy
A Woman that cares about more than just herself

I am living my life like it's Golden
Being real with myself about what I want
Life is too short for regrets
We ALL deserve to be happy

I am living my life like it's Golden
I am not holding on to the past, but looking boldly to
the future
With my head held high like the Queen that I am
I proclaim that this is my time

This is my time to revel in the Woman that I am
This is my time to celebrate the Woman that I am
becoming

I am living my life like it's Golden
Thanking God for everything that he has given to me
It has not always been easy
But I thank God that at the end of every battle I can
count the Victory

I am living my life like it's Golden

Nothing is going to stand in my way
I am destined for Great Things
Destined to have Peace
Destined to have Prosperity
Destined to have and represent Love

Inspiration

Jill Scott's "Golden" – she's just a phenomenal artist! I wanted to write something with the same spirit, energy and grace.

You Are More

Life can be so difficult at times
Long, and seemingly never-ending valleys
Constant struggles – sometimes against others,
sometimes against Self
But through it all
Every disappointment and fear
Every hurdle
Every cry offered in the still of the night

YOU ARE MORE

More than your mistakes
More than the self doubts that creep into your mind
when things don't go quite as planned
More than anything that you have endured

YOU ARE MORE

You are worthy of love
Worthy of compassion
Worthy of success

You were created for a reason
You are wonderfully and perfectly made
There is no one like you in the entire universe
You are a glowing star in a world often void of light
Your life is filled with purpose
You can overcome any obstacle

YOU ARE MORE

You are awesome
Extraordinary
Your purpose is divine

You CANNOT be defeated

Inspiration

This poem was inspired by victims of domestic abuse at a local shelter in Chicago. These women go through so much, and yet they find the strength to endure. I hope that they are happy, loved and safe.

Faithful to You/By Your Side

When the sun runs out I will remain standing by your side
I will be there to protect you from the darkness and storms
Though shadows dance around you, I will NOT let them consume you
Serenity will be granted and everything will be all right

When the sun runs out I will not abandon you
I will not leave you like flotsam adrift on the shore
You can hold on to me and know that normalcy will return

You are so dear to me
I will not leave you to drown in the depth of your fears
I will act as the lighthouse that guides you safely home

When the sun runs out and precious few remain, you are NOT alone
Know that once again you will be bathed in the warmth of the light
Peace will reemerge and through it all I will remain by your side

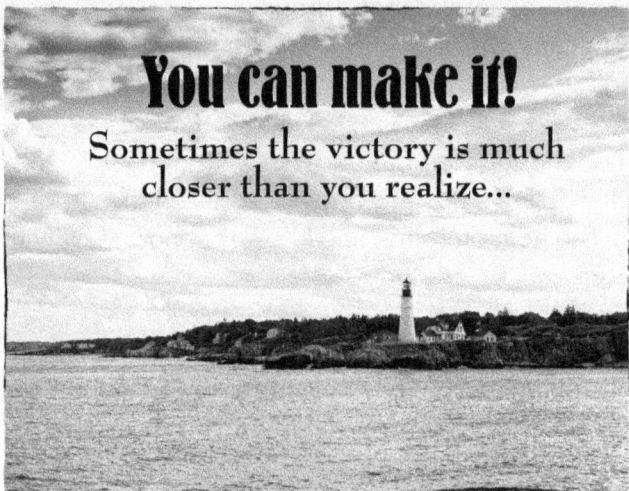

You can make it!

Sometimes the victory is much closer than you realize...

Inspiration

Sometimes people need to know that there is someone in their corner – regardless of how bleak things may appear to be. We all get a little lost at various points in our lives. At times we are able to find the way on our own; in other instances we need a lighthouse to help guide us home.

Baggage

Let everything go
All of the Pain
Disappointments
Expectations
Hurt

Release them.

Let go of the anger
The feelings of inadequacy
Let go of the feelings of aggression and contempt

Forgive them.
Forgive yourself.

You have so much baggage that it's holding you back
You look backwards into the past and in the process
neglect to see the brightness of your future

Stand up.

Stand up to every challenge...
Every naysayer...
Every stumble, and yes, even every fall...

You must stand, even when you are so weary that you
feel you cannot take another step
Stand up

Stand up and leave all of your baggage behind.

Inspiration

We all walk around with a set of experiences that no one can see, but it's there just below the surface. Maybe you have a failed relationship that you never healed from... Maybe you expect way too much of yourself (or others), and those expectations are causing you to fail (or worse yet, to not even try). Whatever the situation, leave all of your baggage behind and enjoy all that life has to offer.

The Beauty of Truth

I see your true Beauty shining through
It's the Beauty of Love, Grace and Compassion

Yes, I see your true beauty shining through
It's there in the way you Smile
It's there in the way we Share
It's there in your Character

I see the Beauty of Truth when I look into your eyes

You are a Woman whose Past has spurred her into the
endless Grace of the Future
A woman with Unlimited Potential....a Life BLESSED
with Boundless Possibilities

I see your true Beauty shining through
Your Wit...
Elegance...
Moral Fiber...
Selflessness...

Everything about you is Beautiful to me

Through the deepest of valleys and the stormiest of
seas, I will be your anchor
When the rays of sunshine fill your life and soul with
JOY, I will exalt and dance beside you

I see the Beauty of Truth when I look into your eyes
I see the TRUE Beauty of you

Inspiration

Amazing friendships! We should let people know how we feel about them each day – through our actions, deeds, words and conversations. **True friendship is sacred, and it should be treated as such...**

Unlimited

I am not afraid to push for what I want
I am not Fearful of battling my Inner Demons...of
pressing towards the LIGHT
Sometimes I do get tired, but I am not afraid to push
through the exhaustion
I am not afraid to FORGIVE...to let go of past hurts
and pain
I am not afraid to LOVE those who would seek to use
or turn my love for them against me
I am not afraid to reach for the Sun and Moon...for
Treasures Seen and UNSEEN
To glory in all of the delights that the Angels are ready
to lay at my feet

I am so GRATEFUL
Grateful for ALL of the Beautiful people that I've met
Grateful for those who have LOVED me as
unconditionally as any Human Being can....
Grateful for the betrayals
Grateful for the rise, the fall and the ability to rise
again
I Am Just GRATEFUL

I do not regret any part of my Journey...any single
Experience

I AM NOT AFRAID OF WHO I AM
I am not perfect, but I am ME...Genuine at all times
I am secure in my IMPERFECTIONS because I am
wonderfully made and just as I should be...
Constantly seeking to improve...

Constantly seeking to become a better person...
I Love the Woman that I WAS, AM and WILL EVOLVE
into
I Greet Her with Joy and wait to see Her Future unfold

I see mountaintops, sunrises and galaxies
I feel energy and bliss from the inner core of my Being
I feel at ONE with myself
I feel at PEACE

I EMBRACE THIS MOMENT, for this moment is
singular
This moment cannot exist again
Tomorrow may never come...but right NOW...right
now I am DANCING
I am dancing into a VORTEX of sun-kissed dew and
brilliant light
I am dancing into LIMITLESS POTENTIAL,
COUNTLESS POSSIBILITIES and NEW HORIZONS

Don't you want to dance, too?
To feel a lightness of Heart, Soul and Spirit
To feel Connected to Yourself so that you can Connect
with Others
Don't you want to DANCE?

Let's go on a journey of discovery together
Unpack your baggage – it's stopping you from
achieving your Destiny
Disappointments and Fears
Discontent
Lack of Faith
Trust issues

All of the DRAMA – real and imagined

Let's get FREE
We need to remove the shackles from our feet so that
we can be FREE

Free to Rejoice in all of the Beauty that surrounds us
Free to live out our Purpose
Free to enjoy this second...this moment in time...this
Gift of Life
Freedom

On the other side of all of our baggage awaits
Immeasurable Joy, Peace and
FREEDOM

Inspiration

Stop trying to please other people and living life according to their rules. Stop trying to prove to others that you are worthy — recognize it for yourself and that simple fact will shine through!

Mantra

I know who I am and it is not defined
by the perceptions of others.

Strut.

When I walk into a room, I don't just step
I don't just glide
I STRUT

I strut with the confidence of a woman who knows
where she's been and is optimistic about where she's
going
I strut with the blood of my forefathers throbbing in
my veins

I strut because my beauty is so much more than skin
deep
My heart is pure and my soul is sure that I am living the
best life that I can possibly live
I am living the type of life that resounds with grace,
humility and love

When I walk into a room, I don't just slink and slide
I strut
I catwalk strut with my head held high, back straight
and a sway to my hips that is second to none

I strut with the love that dwells within me
A love that is born of the love that my Father in
Heaven has bestowed upon me
His love is so awesome and amazing, that I can't do
anything but Strut

And my Friends...my Girls...my fellow Divas...
When we get together, we 'sho nuff' STRUT
Strut with Style, Class, Poise AND Savoir Faire

Me and my Girls
Strut

To the bodacious symphony of saxophones
and the tinkling of ivory keys
We STRUT
Through every success *and* challenge that passes our
way
We STRUT
Through the eye-rolling and blatant jealousy of others
We STRUT
Strut until our eyes sparkle like the rarest of diamonds
with the best kept secret...
Like the greatest queens of the Nile
We STRUT
To do any less than that really is not an option

Inspiration

Life is definitely not a dress rehearsal. Every day should be lived with maximum confidence – head held high, shoulders straight and for those that are so inclined, definitely a little extra sway with the hips! Do not let any situation, person or problem make you walk with your head bowed. You are not subservient, oppressed or down-trodden. Every woman is a QUEEN!

Mountaintop

I have been to the Mountaintop
Caressed words with my fingertips and lips
Felt the syllables burst onto the page as if pulled from
another being
Grappled with the best way to put into words how I
                    F E E L

In the past, I was always so consumed with pleasing
others
But ultimately, it really does not matter what others
say...think...feel about me

I have been to the Mountaintop
Lived moments of grandeur and crawled through the
dark recesses of my Soul
I have danced through the fire, rain and sun
Overcome with emotion as my pen cried out its song
            All in an effort to be at peace with myself
            To accept the uniqueness that was gifted to me

I do not know what the future holds
But it truly does not matter to me
I have been to the Mountaintop

Felt the sweet honeyed caress of the sun from the
inside out
Experienced the wondrous majesty of Love's Embrace
Struggled with how to let go, wrapped in a cloak of
denial
Yearning to be free from a trap made of my own
design

I have touched the Mountaintop

Seen visions of Grace and Mercy dancing in a river
that COVERS me with bliss
I have been to the Mountaintop - with all of its ridges,
valleys, peaks and summits
I have been to the MOUNTAINTOP
My heart is filled with Joy

Inspiration

In life we frequently encounter obstacles. Often, it is not so much the difficulty of the problem that determines the end result, but how we choose to react to the problem(s) – reactive versus resolving! The next time things do not go quite as planned, center yourself; give yourself a moment to think calmly and logically about whatever the issue is that you are facing. You can go to the Mountaintop and be victorious, as opposed to dwelling in the valley of defeat!

UniverSOUL

I believe that Energy is Universal
There is Magic pulsing through our veins
So much power resides within US

We each have the chance to make a difference

There is more to life than monetary gains and material
things
Compassion
Friendships
Thankfulness

The truth is we each have a chance to make a
difference
We each have an opportunity to make sure that our
lives benefit more than just us

This life is a Beautiful Gift
We are living separate lives, yet we are not alone
Every action we undertake affects the life of someone
else

Our experiences are distinct, but they are not different
At the core we are more Connected than we realize
Transmitting and receiving energy...both good and
bad
Often unknowingly affecting those we interact with
on a daily basis...for better or worse

In so many ways we are ONE
And yes, the energy we create is UniverSOUL

Inspiration

The way that we treat each other matters! Be kind, loving, compassionate and generous. Be gentle with yourself *and* others!

Beautiful

I am surrounded by Love, Joy and Peace
There is no regret about the direction that my life has
taken
All of these collective experiences – triumphs,
mistakes, downfalls, successes
They are pieces of the puzzle that have served to
make me who I am
I am in sync with Nature...flowing with Grace,
Maturity and Self-Assurance

The planets and constellations have been laid at my
feet
I am walking into a Universe filled with Unlimited
Possibilities

Though problems do exist, I do not feel stressed

I am filled with an abundance of Gratitude
Honored by the individuals that are a part of my life
Blessed beyond measure

I have PEACE in my SOUL and Happiness in my Heart
I am LOVED
I am loved BEYOND MEASURE

I just want to give back all that has been given to me
To be a beautiful and awesome representation of all
the blessings that have been bestowed upon me

I want to leave a legacy of Grace, Compassion and
LOVE

To be known for giving of myself just for the love of it...not for an expected return

I just want to represent LOVE

Inspiration

Love, grace and mercy.

Mantra

I embrace this moment.
I am open to all opportunities for growth.
I am loved and represent love.

PHAT.

i am phat.

I am Word and Sound and LIFE
I Breathe Positive Energy into Negative Situations
I am FIERCE, Loyal and Strong
I am not Afraid to Push beyond Obstacles
Not Too Protective of Self to Burst through Concrete
and Jump Over Hurdles
I SMASH thoughts of Self Defeat

i AM phat.

I Am ALL that *and* SOME
I Am Movement and Vibration and LYRICISM
I Attack Doubt and Fear with FEROCITY
I Multiply Beats, Rhymes and ENERGY

i am PHAT.

I am Focused
Divine
A Queen
In Love With Myself, and thus CAPABLE of Loving
OTHERS

I am phat.

I transform syllables into Words
I Birth Life and Imagery into my VERSES
I AM POETRY in Motion

I Am Art

Constantly Flowing...Changing...Evolving
I AM the Phoneix Rising From the Flames
I Am One with the WORDS
I Am the Caged Bird that Finally Learned How to Sing

I Am An Imperfect Being Destined For Great Things.

PHAT.

Inspiration

Learning to walk in my greatness...

Metamorphosis

I feel kissed by the Sun
Do you know how it feels to go through a Genesis?
To be in touch with the very depths of your being?
How it feels to dance into the LIGHT...away from the
Darkness and pitfalls?
Away from the traps that in many instances, You laid
for You...

Do you know how it feels to be at Perfect Peace with
yourself?
How it feels to LOVE YOU...and all of the
imperfections that make you, YOU?

It feels like pure ENERGY
Like anything and everything is possible

It feels like boundless JOY
Like swimming in the waters of BLISS

Do you know how it feels to begin to Walk In Your
Greatness?

Inspiration

Gratitude for everything that is me.

Life is full of unlimited possibilities...

A Dance of Freedom

(Final Thoughts)

I have danced into a kaleidoscope of color
Everything feels New
I Feel New
If I had to choose one word to describe this feeling, it
would be Freedom
A lightness of soul, heart and mind
And yes...FREEDOM

This life is a journey. Along the way we encounter people, places, situations and tasks that are meant to challenge and strengthen us. I never thought that I would write a book of poetry. For a multitude of reasons, I never thought that what I needed to express was worth sharing.

From this day forward I want you, the reader, to begin to explore **every talent that has been bestowed upon you.** Don't be afraid to try. Don't be afraid to live... Let's go on a journey of opportunity and exploration together!

Love, Peace and Blessings,
Kimberly

Acknowledgements

Heather Pettersen – Each time I see "Dancing in the Sun", my heart sings! **Thank you for the amazing painting that serves as my cover.** For more information on Heather and her works of art, please visit www.heatherpettersen.com.

Kevin A. Sutton – You are my brother and friend. For as long as I can remember, you have done everything within your power to support my dreams and endeavors. I know that this is not the type of book you had in mind, but this is a dream come true for me... Thank you, Kevin. You have left an indelible mark on my life that cannot possibly be expressed in words.

Jolynn C. Caroline – God really blessed me the day that He allowed our paths to cross. You are kind-hearted, driven, focused and extremely intelligent. But more than that, you are my friend. Any time I have *ever* needed you, you have been there. Our friendship has changed my life for nothing but the better. I truly could not ask for a better friend.

Michelle Seals – I feel like you really get me. I am prone to being eccentric, over-emotional and somewhat demanding. You know all that about me, and you choose to be Best Friends with me anyway. Thank you for the gift of your friendship.

Khalilah Harmon and Youmna El – I appreciate the time, energy and effort that you each put into reviewing my "baby". Thank you for being my unofficial co-editors.

Kimmah Shah and **Akilah Nisa Scott** – You changed my life! Thank you for helping me to lose some excess baggage. Without you, I would not have been free to dance into unlimited possibilities.

Levon L. Wilson – Thank you for nurturing my love of music. So much of my poetry is inspired by music. Sometimes I wonder if the way that I hear certain phrases or artists would be the same had we not become friends. When I met you I enjoyed music, but through our friendship music became a fire that burned in my soul. In particular, you introduced me to hip-hop on a completely different level! I know that it took me a long time to share that with you, but it's true. Thank you for sharing your love of music with me.

Relana Johnson – Editor. Sounding Board. Partner-In-Editing and Event Planning Crime. You took my phoenix and turned it into flames! Thank you, Relana.

Elijah, Jakob, Jeremy and Jordan Sutton – I love you guys so much! Whenever I see you I think of unlimited potential AND possibilities. Please always remember that if you're willing to put in the work, you can do, be and achieve anything that you desire. Auntie Kim loves you!

Reflections

Journaling our thoughts is a sure-fire way to confirm that the lives we see in our minds are truly the lives that we are experiencing.

Consider the following:

✿ Who and what inspires you?
✿ What do you believe in?
✿ What holds value in your life?
✿ Are there any fears that have held you back from pursuing a dream...if so, what are you going to do to let go of the fear(s)?

Let your pen act as your mouthpiece - it will take you on journeys that you never dared to imagine.

REFLECTIONS

REFLECTIONS

REFLECTIONS

REFLECTIONS

REFLECTIONS

PHOTOGRAPHY CREDITS

Section I
Mouse209, *Inner cathedral.* Pixmac

Yannis, *Faith* (2650m)

Section II
Popsicles, Library of Congress, Prints & Photographs Division, FSA-OWI Collection, [reproduction number, e.g., LC-USF35-1326]

Carla Vasquez, *Unity*

Vos Efx, *Hat*

Steve Snodgrass, *Power & Equality*

Section III
Jasleen Kaur, *Gradientheart*. Pixmac

Steve Richard, Heart of stone

edenpictures (Eden, Janine and Jim), Double Dutch II

Stephen A. Wolfe, *Violinists*

Section IV
Kozzi, *Road with Snow*

Stephen A. Wolfe, South Beach 5 (Explored)

Motoko Henusaki (Moto猫), Mountaintop

Yasin Hassan, *Sunday means get together*

www.ingramcontent.com/pod-product-compliance
Lightning Source LLC
Chambersburg PA
CBHW020854090426
42736CB00008B/371